The Bridge to the New Testament

A Comprehensive Guide to the Forgotten Years of the Inter-Testament Period

Question and Answer Guide

Denny Sissom

Testament Press, LLC
P.O. Box 5593
Huntsville, AL 35814

TheBridgeToTheNewTestament.com
TestamentPress.com

ISBN: 978-1-7333756-4-1 (Paperback)
ISBN: 978-1-7333756-5-8 (Digital)

This answer book is the companion to
*The Bridge to the New Testament: A Comprehensive Guide
to the Forgotten Years of the Inter-Testament Period:*

ISBN: 978-1-7333756-1-0 (Hardback)
ISBN: 978-1-7333756-2-7 (Paperback)
ISBN: 978-1-7333756-3-4 (Digital)

Printed in the United States of America

Table of Contents

Chapter 1
▪ Introduction ▪

1. How many books of the Bible are there? 66
2. Approximately how many men wrote the Bible? 40
3. In what three languages was the Bible originally written? Hebrew, Aramaic, and Greek
4. On what three continents did Bible events take place? Europe, Asia, and Africa
5. From Figure 1-2, when did Roman rule begin in Judea? 63 BC
6. What event marked the beginning of the Christian age? The crucifixion of Jesus
7. Approximately how long of a period did the New Testament cover, at least as defined in this book? 101 years
8. From Figure 1-2, explain the difference between the solid line at the end of the northern kingdom of Israel and the dotted line at the end of the southern kingdom of Judah. Israel was destroyed and never returned while Judah returned from captivity
9. What event marked the end of the Patriarchal Age? The Israelites crossing the Red Sea
10. Approximately how many years encompassed the inter-testament period? 420 years
11. What was the dominant world empire at the end of the Old Testament? Persian Empire
12. What was the dominant world empire at the beginning of the New Testament? Roman Empire
13. What are the last three historical books of the Old Testament? Ezra, Nehemiah, and Esther
14. In general, what language mix was there in Judea at the end of the Old Testament? Aramaic and Hebrew
15. In general, what language mix was there in Judea at the beginning of the New Testament? Aramaic and Greek
16. Name three things that are in the New Testament that arose during the inter-testament period. Herod's Temple, synagogues, Sadducees, and Pharisees
17. Who was responsible for spreading Greek culture to the known world during the inter-testament period? Alexander the Great

18. Which two generals of Alexander the Great (and their successors) had the most influence on the Palestinian region? Ptolemy I Soter and Seleucus I Nicator
19. Who offered a pig on the Temple altar during the inter-testament period? Antiochus IV Epiphanes
20. What is the only Jewish feast/festival to have begun during the inter-testament period? Hanukkah, or the Festival of Lights
21. What does *apocrypha* mean? Hidden or secret
22. In what language was the Septuagint written? Greek
23. What Jewish institution established in the inter-testament period (or perhaps late in the Old Testament period) is the model for our church buildings today? Synagogues
24. What was the name of the Jewish high court? Sanhedrin
25. What two time-keeping instruments were available during the inter-testament period? Sundials and water clocks
26. How many hours were in a Roman day (daylight hours) and how do they differ from our hours today? Twelve and they were evenly divided over the period of daylight
27. In Jerusalem during the time of Jesus, how long would the shortest hour have been and how long would the longest have been? 50.37 min, 71.14 min
28. How many days did the Roman week have during the inter-testament and New Testament periods? Eight
29. Why is "Wednesday" spelled funny? Because it is named after the Anglo-Saxon god Woden and from the Old English "Wodnesdaeg"
30. After what Roman god was Saturday named? Saturn
31. When does a Jewish day start? At twilight (when three stars appear in the night sky), or more specifically, the approximate end of civil twilight)
32. Upon what Biblical reason does the Jewish day begin? During creation when days were denoted by *"and there was evening and there was morning"*
33. What is another term that often denotes major Jewish holidays? High Sabbaths
34. What is the only Jewish day of the week that has a name? The Sabbath
35. What are the three different twilight names? Civil, Nautical, and Astronomical

36. Explain two reasons why biblical chronologies are complicated. Reigns of kings overlap and the difference between solar and lunar calendars

37. Give two examples of why the rotation of the earth is slowing. Earthquakes and tidal friction

38. What calendar came into effect for the Roman Republic in 46 BC? The Julian calendar

39. What is the name of the calendar system we use today? The Gregorian calendar

40. Which months did not exist in the lunar calendar created by Romulus? January and February

41. To what name was the month of Quintilus changed, and in whose honor was it done? July in honor of Julius Caesar

42. To what name was the month of Sextilis changed, and in whose honor was it done? August in honor of Caesar Augustus

43. Who was initially responsible for adding leap years every four years to the calendar, thus making it repeat every four years? Julius Caesar

44. Who modified the leap years from being every four years by omitting three leap years out of every 400 years? Pope Gregory XIII

45. What year and month had exactly three weeks? October 1582

46. What was the last European country to accept the Gregorian calendar and what year did they accept it? Greece in 1923

47. Since *octo* means eight, why is October (our tenth month) named the way it is? Because octo was the eighth month in the original Roman calendar of ten months

48. When various countries originally accepted the Gregorian calendar in October of 1582, what date followed October 4? October 15

49. When Britain and its American colonies finally adopted the Gregorian calendar, what date followed September 2, 1752? September 14

50. To synchronize the Jewish lunar calendar with the seasons of the year, how often was Adar I added? Seven times every 19 years

51. What number needs to be added to the Gregorian year to get the equivalent Jewish year? 3761

52. When were the *Kalends* on the Roman calendar? The first of the month

53. **When were the *Nones* on the Roman calendar?** The fifth of the month on 29-day months (Jan, April, June, Aug., Sept, Nov, Dec, and also February) and the seventh of the month on 31-day months (March, May, July, and October)
54. **When were the *Ides* on the Roman calendar?** The thirteenth of the month on 29-day months (Jan, April, June, Aug., Sept, Nov, Dec, and also February) and the fifteenth of the month on 31-day months (March, May, July, and October)
55. **Did the Romans count days before the three fixed points (*Kalends*, *Nones*, and *Ides*) or did they count days after these points?** Before
56. **In the calendar of Numa Pompilius, what would be the date for Prid. Non. October?** October 6
57. **In the calendar of Numa Pompilius, what would be the Roman equivalent of November 23?** A.d. VIII Kal. December
58. **What year between 1 BC and AD 1 does not exist?** The year 0
59. **In the Tishri-years Jewish calendar, which month is number five?** Shevat
60. **What Jewish month aligns with March-April?** Nisan
61. **Which dispensation (or age) overlapped the Old, Inter, and New Testaments?** Mosaic

Chapter 2
▪ Old Testament History Review ▪

1. From which of Noah's sons—Shem, Ham or Japheth—did Abraham descend? Shem
2. Which two "tribes of Israel" were not sons of Jacob? Manasseh and Ephraim
3. Which two sons of Jacob were not "tribes of Israel"? Joseph and Levi
4. Through what grandson of Abraham was he the "father of the Jews"? Jacob (Israel)
5. Through what son of his was Abraham the "father of the Arabs"? Ishmael
6. From what great-grandson of Abraham did Jesus descend? Judah
7. Who was the favorite son of Jacob? Joseph
8. By which of Abraham's brothers was Lot Abraham's nephew? Haran
9. Who was the only daughter born to Jacob? Dinah
10. What was Jacob's other name? Israel
11. How long were the Israelites in Egypt? 430 years
12. How long did the Israelites wander in the desert before entering the Promised Land? 40 years
13. Which two spies gave a favorable report on the Israelite's ability to conquer Canaan? Joshua and Caleb
14. Which two people over twenty years old were allowed to enter Canaan? Joshua and Caleb
15. How many cities of refuge were set up after the conquest of Canaan? Six
16. How many cities did the Levites have reserved for them? 48
17. How many major cycles are in the book of Judges? Seven
18. What were the five distinct events that happened during each cycle? Sin, Servitude, Repentance, Salvation, and Rest
19. Name three kingdoms the Israelites would have to serve during the period of the judges. Philistines, Midianites, Ammonites
20. Who was the last judge *mentioned* in the book of Judges? Samson
21. Who was the last judge, who was also a prophet and established the Israelite monarchy? Samuel

22. Which two of Samuel's sons caused the people to want a king? Joel and Abijah
23. Who was the first king of the united kingdom of Israel and how long did he reign? Saul, 40 years
24. When David first became king, which part of the nation did he rule and for how long? Judah for 7 ½ years
25. How long did David rule over the whole kingdom? Just over 40 years
26. Which son of Saul became king over a portion of the kingdom after the death of his father? Ishbaal
27. Which of David's wives bore Solomon? Bathsheba
28. For what construction project is Solomon most famous? The Temple
29. Why did God divide the kingdom upon the death of Solomon? Because of Solomon's foreign wives and his adoption of some of their practices
30. Who was the first king over the divided kingdom in the north? Jeroboam
31. Who was the first king over the divided kingdom in the south? Rehoboam
32. What was the name of the northern kingdom? Israel
33. What was the name of the southern kingdom? Judah
34. How many tribes went to the northern kingdom? Ten
35. Which king of Israel only reigned for seven days? Zimri
36. Who was the last king of Israel? Hoshea
37. In what year was Israel destroyed and by which nation? 721 BC, by Assyria
38. Who was the last king of Judah? Zedekiah
39. In what year was Judah destroyed and by which nation? 586 BC, by the Babylonians
40. How did the Samaritans come about where the northern kingdom of Israel used to be? They were an intermixed group of the remnants of the ten tribes of Israel and other displaced peoples, including Assyrians
41. What event does Jeremiah lament in the first part of Lamentations chapter 4? The attack on Jerusalem
42. In what year was Daniel carried into captivity in Babylon? 606 BC
43. In what year did the Babylonians destroy the Temple? 586 BC

44. Approximately how long of a period was between the destruction of the first Temple and the beginning of construction of the second Temple? About 50 years
45. Why did the synagogues become the place of worship for the Jews during the Babylonian captivity? The Temple had been destroyed and the Jews needed places to worship
46. Which kingdom was the chest and arms of silver in Nebuchadnezzar's dream? Medo-Persians
47. Which Persian king issued a decree around 538 BC to allow the Jews to return to their homeland? Cyrus
48. Under whose leadership, after the return to Jerusalem, was the Temple rebuilt? Zerubbabel
49. About how many people returned to Jerusalem from captivity the first time? Approximately 50,000
50. Under whose leadership were the walls of Jerusalem rebuilt? Nehemiah
51. Name two other "notable people" living in the world the first time the Jews returned to Judea. Confucius and Buddha

Chapter 3
▪ The Greek Empire ▪

1. Chapters 2, 7, and 8 of the book of Daniel recount the dream of Nebuchadnezzar and two visions of Daniel. Which vision (which chapter of Daniel) did not cover the Babylonian or Roman kingdoms (hint: look back at Table 2-2)? Daniel 8

2. In Daniel's dream of Daniel 8, which kingdom was the ram with two horns? Medo-Persians

3. In Daniel's dream of Daniel 8, which kingdom was the male goat? Greece

4. In Daniel's dream of Daniel 8, who was the little horn that sprang from the others? When did he rule over Judea? Antiochus IV Epiphanes, 175-167 BC

5. In Daniel's dream of Daniel 8, what period does the 2,300 evenings and mornings represent? From the first incursion into Jerusalem by Antiochus IV Epiphanes in 170 BC to the restoration of the Temple in 164 BC

6. In what year did Alexander the Great die and how old was he when he died? In 323 BC at the age of 32

7. Which three significant periods spanned the inter-testament period (Figure 3-1)? The Persian period, the Hellenistic period, and the Roman period

8. During inter-testament times, what five kingdoms/rulers composed the Hellenistic period? The Greeks, Ptolemies, Seleucids, Maccabees and Hasmoneans

9. What event started the Hellenistic period? When Alexander the Great took control of Judea

10. In what year did the Roman period begin? 63 BC

11. What incident began the Roman period? Pompey invaded Judea

12. About what year did the Old Testament end? Around 425 BC

13. About what year did the New Testament begin? Around 6 BC

14. What Persian king ruled Judea at the end of the Old Testament? Artaxerxes

15. Who was the last Persian king to rule Judea? Darius III

16. Which part of Greece is now an island due to the construction of a canal in the late 1800's? The Peloponnese

17. Where does Greece rank in a list of the "longest coastlines in the world?" Tenth
18. What was the Greek name for the city-state? Polis
19. Who was the leader of the 300 Spartans who stood up to the Persian army at Thermopylae in 480 BC? Leonidas
20. Between what two Greek city-states were the Peloponnesian Wars? Sparta and Athens
21. From what did the Peloponnesian Wars get their name? From the Peloponnesian region
22. In what year did the Peloponnesian Wars end and who was the victor? 404 BC, Sparta was victorious
23. What man united Greece and the city-states? Philip II
24. What was a *phalanx*? A body of troops that move in close formation
25. At what river did Alexander the Great first defeat the Persians? The Granicus River
26. In what year did Alexander the Great peacefully take Jerusalem? 332 BC
27. What was the name of the high priest at the time Alexander took Jerusalem who stood by his promises to King Darius III no matter the cost? Jaddua
28. What is the term for the embracing of pro-Greek culture? Hellenism
29. Compare and contrast a good characteristic and a bad characteristic of Alexander the Great. One of the greatest leaders the world has ever known, but he gave no thought of who would succeed him
30. Who was the first Samaritan high priest? Manasseh
31. Describe the events that led to the building of the Samaritan temple on Mt. Gerizim. Manasseh, the brother of the high priest Jaddua, wanted to stay married to his foreign wife against the will of the Jews. So Manasseh's father-in-law promised to build Manasseh a temple in Samaria.
32. What was the first Samaritan high priest's relationship to the Jewish high priest? They were brothers
33. Name at least four ways that Alexander the Great could have died. Poisoned, overdose of medication, alcoholism, disease
34. Who was the only known son of Alexander the Great? Alexander IV

35. What two relatives of Alexander ruled as "co-kings" shortly after the death of Alexander the Great, despite that neither was fit to rule? Philip Arrhidaeus and Alexander IV

36. Why were neither of the "co-kings" fit to serve in a decision-making capacity? His half-brother, Philip Arrhidaeus, was mentally unfit, and his son, Alexander IV, was an infant

37. Both of the "co-kings" that ruled after Alexander the Great had a regent that served as the actual decision maker for the kingdom. Who was the first principal Regent (who lived beyond a few weeks) under these two "co-kings"? Perdiccas

38. Since none of Alexander's successors was resilient enough to take control of the empire, approximately how many *total* rulers ruled the kingdom formerly ruled by Alexander the Great? 20 or more

39. Who best exemplified the philosophy of keeping Alexander's kingdom intact under the kingship of Alexander's blood relatives? Perdiccas

40. What sparked the first Diadochi War? When Ptolemy I took the body of Alexander the Great back to Egypt to be buried at Alexandria

41. Alexander's kingdom was divided into four major parts a few years after his death. Who were the four generals that controlled these major provinces from about 317-312 BC? Cassander, Ptolemy I, Lysimachus, and Antigonus I

42. Who were the four generals of Alexander's that controlled the major regions of his divided kingdom from 297-287 BC? Ptolemy I Soter, Lysimachus, Seleucus I Nicator, Demetrius I

43. Who are the four people most often considered being the "four horns" as written about in Daniel, Chapter 8? Cassander, Ptolemy I Soter, Lysimachus, and Seleucus I Nicator

Chapter 4
▪ The Ptolemaic Empire ▪

1. Name one reason the history of the Ptolemies is complicated. Because most of them were named Ptolemy (or Cleopatra)
2. When did control of Judea first pass to the Ptolemies? 323 BC
3. Under which Ptolemaic ruler did the ultimate control of Coele-Syria pass from the Ptolemies to the Seleucids? Ptolemy V Epiphanes
4. In what year did the ultimate control of Coele-Syria pass from the Ptolemies to the Seleucids? 198 BC
5. Whose daughter (one of the *Diadochi*) was Eurydice, Ptolemy I Soter's wife? Antipater
6. Whose daughter (one of the *Diadochi*) was Arsinoe I, Ptolemy II Philadelphus's wife? Lysimachus
7. Why did Coele-Syria have to endure so much of the conflict between the Ptolemies and the Seleucids? Because of its geographic location between the Ptolemaic and Seleucid Empires
8. Who stole the body of Alexander the Great after he died and where did he take it? Ptolemy I took it to Memphis, Egypt
9. Where did the body of Alexander the Great finally end up sometime after 282 BC and who had it moved? Alexandria, Ptolemy II Philadelphus
10. Which of the Ptolemaic rulers was a bodyguard of Alexander the Great? Ptolemy I
11. In what capacity did Ptolemy I Soter rule Egypt from 323-305 BC? In what capacity from 305-282 BC? Satrap (governor) at first, then King
12. How did Ptolemy I Soter treat the Jews *at first* and what did he do? He treated them badly and took over Jerusalem on a Sabbath day
13. What famous mathematician did Ptolemy I sponsor? Euclid
14. In whose reign was the Septuagint *completed*? Ptolemy III Euergetes
15. If Ptolemy IX Soter II were to introduce his mother, two wives, and one of his daughters, what simple way could he introduce them? All as Cleopatra

16. Name the three husbands of Cleopatra VII. Ptolemy XIII, Ptolemy XIV, and Mark Antony

17. Who was the only Cleopatra to marry three times, none of whom was a Ptolemy? Cleopatra Thea

18. Besides being his wife, in what other two ways was Cleopatra III related to Ptolemy VIII? She was his stepdaughter and niece

19. Which Ptolemy commissioned the Septuagint, which was a translation of the Old Testament from Aramaic to Greek? Ptolemy II Philadelphus

20. As a whole, did the first three Ptolemies act favorably toward the Jews or treat them badly? Acted favorably toward

21. Which Ptolemaic ruler attempted to enter the Holy of Holies in the Jewish temple? Ptolemy IV Philopater

22. During the ruling career of Ptolemy VI Philometor, with which family members did he reign? With his mother, Cleopatra I; with his wife/sister, Cleopatra II, and his brother, Ptolemy VIII Physcon; then with one of his sons for a very short time, Ptolemy Eupator; and then possibly with Ptolemy VII Neos Philopater (if not the same person as Ptolemy Eupator)

23. By whom was Cleopatra III Philometor killed and how was her murderer related to her? Her son, Ptolemy X

24. How long did Berenice III rule with her husband, Ptolemy XI Alexander II? 19 days

25. Who were Ptolemy XV Caesarion's famous parents? Julius Caesar and Cleopatra VII Philopator

26. Who were the four people that the *famous* Cleopatra VII (the one that married Mark Antony) ruled jointly with during her career? With her father, Ptolemy XII; with (and later in opposition to) her brother/husband Ptolemy XIII; with her brother/husband Ptolemy XIV; and with her son Ptolemy XV Caesarion

27. To whom did Cleopatra VII rule in opposition during her career? Ptolemy XIII at one time and both Ptolemy XIII and Arsinoe IV at a later time

28. Who commissioned the Rosetta stone? Ptolemy V Epiphanes

29. In what three forms of writing is the Rosetta stone inscribed, and why is this important? Ancient Egyptian hieroglyphics, demotic script, and ancient Greek; it helped unravel how to read ancient Egyptian hieroglyphics

30. Where is the Rosetta stone now? The British Museum

31. What was the nationality of the woman that began the famous line of Egyptian queens named Cleopatra? Syrian, or Seleucid
32. What was the nationality of the man that began the famous line of Egyptian kings named Ptolemy? Greek/Macedonian
33. Control of Egypt temporarily passed to the Seleucids in 168 BC during the reign of Ptolemy VI Philometor. Who was the Seleucid king that took control? Antiochus IV Ephiphanes
34. When Cleopatra VII Philopator attempted to make her brother/husband subordinate to her, he became sole ruler due to the backlash of their subjects. Who was this brother/husband of hers? Ptolemy XIII
35. Which Ptolemy ordered the beheading of the great Roman leader Pompey in front of his wife and children? Ptolemy XIII
36. Who was the enemy of Pompey that was infuriated with this Ptolemy (see question 35) for having Pompey killed? Julius Caesar
37. How did Cleopatra VII seize upon the opportunity presented by the beheading of Pompey? She offered herself to Caesar
38. Who is typically recognized to be the last of the Ptolemies to rule before Rome took over Egypt, even though her son outlived her by a short time? Cleopatra VII Philopator
39. After Julius Caesar was assassinated in 44 BC, what three men formed the second Roman triumvirate? Mark Antony, Marcus Aemilius Lepidus, and Octavian
40. What did Octavian have the opportunity to do when Mark Antony moved to Alexandria and married Cleopatra VII Philopator in 37 BC? He convinced the Roman Senate to declare war on Cleopatra
41. What decisive sea battle in September of 31 BC decided the ultimate fate of Cleopatra VII and Mark Antony? The battle of Actium, off the coast of western Greece
42. When Antony heard that Cleopatra VII was dead, how did he try to kill himself? He stabbed himself in the stomach with his sword
43. Who considered killing Cleopatra VII for Antony's sake? Herod the Great
44. How many Caesar's were "one too many" for Octavian? Two

Chapter 5
▪ The Seleucid Empire ▪

1. In what year did control of Coele-Syria finally pass from the Ptolemies to the Seleucids? 198 BC
2. Which Seleucid king took control of Coele-Syria at this time? Antiochus III the Great
3. Into what five provinces was Coele-Syria sectioned at this time? Judea, Samaria, Galilee, Perea, and Trachonitis
4. Who was the founder of the Seleucid Empire? Seleucus I Nicator
5. How many Syrian wars were there, and what two nations were at war? Six, Syria and Egypt
6. Between what two parties was the treaty of Apamea? Syria (Antiochus III the Great) and Rome
7. Who invaded Greece to cause the treaty of Apamea? Antiochus III the Great
8. In whose reign did the Maccabean revolt take place? Antiochus IV Epiphanes
9. Who claimed to be the adopted son of Antiochus IV Epiphanes? Alexander Balas
10. Which Seleucid king ruled for two distinct periods? Demetrius II Nicator
11. Name four non-bloodline Seleucid rulers that *did not* claim to be a son of another king that ruled the kingdom. Lysias, Heliodorus, Diodotus Tryphon, and Tigranes II
12. Name two non-blood-line Seleucid rulers who claimed to be sons of former Seleucid kings. Alexander Balas and Alexander II Zabinas
13. Who claimed to be the adopted son of Antiochus VII? Alexander II Zabinas
14. Who was married to three different Seleucid kings and was the "matriarch" of the later Seleucid kingdom civil wars? Cleopatra Thea
15. Who killed his mother after she tried to kill him with poisoned wine? Antiochus VIII Grypus
16. Which Seleucid ruler was more like a mayor than a king? Seleucus VII Philometor

17. Who took over the entire Seleucid Empire in 83 BC, and from where did he come? Tigranes II, from Armenia
18. Name two connections between the bloodlines of the Ptolemies and the Seleucids. Cleopatra Thea and Tryphaena
19. What were the names of the three "foreigners" that Cleopatra V Selene married? Antiochus VIII Grypus, Antiochus IX Cyzicenus, and Antiochus X Eusebus Philopator
20. Who were the five sons of Antiochus VIII Grypus? Seleucus VI Epiphanes Nicator, Philip I Philadelphus, Antiochus XI Epiphanes Philadelphus, Demetrius III Eucaerus, and Antiochus XII Dionysus
21. In what year did Seleucus I Nicator declare himself king? 305 BC
22. In 301 BC, Seleucus I Nicator founded the new capital of the Syrian Empire. After whom was it named? Antioch, named after his father, Antiochus
23. What was the full name of the daughter of Antiochus III the Great that became the namesake for many of the Ptolemaic queens until the end of that empire? Cleopatra I Syra
24. How many attempts did it take for Antiochus III the Great to finally gain control of Coele-Syria from the Ptolemies? Five
25. Who was the famous son of Antiochus III the Great held hostage by Rome for twelve years? Antiochus IV Epiphanes
26. When Heliodorus went to Jerusalem to rob the Temple of its treasure, what stopped him, according to II Maccabees 3:25-26? "A magnificently caparisoned horse with a rider of frightening mien."
27. When Antiochus IV Epiphanes returned from his captivity in Rome, who was sent in his place to become the new hostage? Demetrius I Soter
28. What name did the Jews give Antiochus IV Epiphanes? Antiochus IV Epimanes
29. Antiochus IV Epiphanes replaced Onias III as high priest with Onias's Hellenized brother. What was this brother's name? Jason
30. With whom did Antiochus IV Epiphanes later replace Onias's brother as high priest? Menelaus
31. Of what Jewish tribe was this high priest in question 30? Benjamin

32. When Antiochus IV Epiphanes was on the verge of total conquest of Egypt, what Roman ambassador stopped him cold? Gaius Popillius Laenas

33. When Antiochus IV Epiphanes sent Apollonius to teach the Jews a lesson, how many Jews did he kill on a Sabbath day when they chose not to defend themselves? 40,000

34. Name four horrible things that Antiochus Epiphanes did to the Jews. Threw two mothers from the city walls, butchered a mother and her seven children, desecrated the Temple by offering a sow on the altar and smearing the broth throughout, and flogged an aged scribe to death because he refused to eat swine

35. How old was Antiochus V Eupator when Demetrius I Soter, his half-brother, killed him? Eleven

36. For what reason was the reign of Demetrius II Nicator broken into two parts? He was taken captive by the Parthians

37. Which two Seleucid king's descendants caused civil war to become common during the later portion of the Seleucid Empire? Demetrius II Nicator and Antiochus IX Cyzicenus

38. Which marriage of Cleopatra Thea did not influence the later civil wars of the Seleucids? Her marriage to Alexander Balas

39. Who was the last ruler of the Seleucid kingdom who ruled from 64-63 BC? Philip II Philoromaeus

40. Who was the only Seleucid king to rule jointly with a relative, in opposition to a relative, and as a sole ruler? Antiochus VIII Grypus

41. Which Roman general finally defeated Tigranes II of Armenia? Pompey

42. Did this Roman general allow Tigranes II to remain on the throne? If so, in what capacity? Yes, as a Roman ally

43. During which Syrian War did the Battle of Raphia take place? The fourth

44. During which Syrian War did the "Day of Eleusis" take place? The sixth

45. Which Syrian War was it that Antiochus III the Great took the ultimate control of Coele-Syria? The fifth

46. Which Syrian War was also known as the Laodicean War? The third

47. Who was the wife of Antiochus II Theos killed by Laodice I, thus starting the Third Syrian War, and who was her brother? Berenice, Ptolemy III Euergetes

48. Which of the early Seleucid kings married his stepmother?
    Antiochus I Soter
49. Among all the Ptolemies and Seleucids, who married the largest number of her brothers, and how many were there that she married? Laodice IV, three
50. What was the name of the decisive battle when Antiochus III the Great gained control of Coele-Syria? The Battle of Panium

Chapter 6
▪ The Maccabean Period ▪

1. From where does the name "Maccabee" come? From Judas's nickname, Maccabeus, which means "the hammer"
2. Who was the father of the Maccabee brothers? Mattathias
3. Where do we learn most of our information regarding the Maccabee brothers? From I and II Maccabees
4. From what event does the Jewish tradition of Hanukkah (Feast of Lights) come? From the re-dedication of the Temple in 164 BC by Judas and the Jews
5. How long is the feast of Hanukkah? Eight days
6. In what battle was Judas killed? The battle of Elasa
7. To what three Seleucid kings was Cleopatra Thea married? Alexander Balas, Demetrius II, and Antiochus VII Sidetes
8. Explain why neither John (first son of Mattathias) nor Eleazar (fourth son of Mattathias) have numbers next to them on Figure 6-1, as the other sons of Mattathias do. Eleazar was killed in 162 BC during the battle of Beth-Zechariah when the elephant he stabbed fell on him, and the Nabataeans killed John in 160 BC
9. Which Maccabee brother was known as the great warrior? Judas
10. Which Maccabee brother was known as the great diplomat? Jonathan
11. In what town did the fight for Jewish independence begin with Mattathias? Modein
12. After Mattathias died, which of his sons (by birth order) led the freedom fighters? What was his name? The third son, Judas
13. Who was the second leader (Maccabean brother) of the revolt and what number of Mattathias's son was he? Jonathan, the fifth son
14. Who was the third leader (Maccabean brother) of the revolt and what number of Mattathias's son was he? Simon, the first son
15. What were the three periods of Judas's battles and what were the numbers (from the table) associated with each? First–

Defensive, battles 3-6; Second–Offensive, battles 7-18; and Third–Defensive, battles 19-24

16. If you examine the blue sidebar summary boxes (the one for each person that shows his mother/father/wives, etc.) for the Maccabees and compare those to the blue sidebar summary boxes for the Seleucids/Ptolemies, you will notice one nuance between the two. From the perspective of the Jews, what is this difference? Rulers vs. leaders

17. Which of Mattathias's sons has become known as "the beast sticker"? Eleazar

18. What fortified area in Jerusalem was besieged at one time or another by all three Maccabee brothers? The Akra

19. Who was the first person killed (by Mattathias) in the fight for Jewish independence? A timid Jew who was going to do what the Syrians wanted

20. What event caused Mattathias to realize that if the Jews continued with this tradition/commandment, there would no longer be a Jewish race? What was the tradition/commandment? When the 1,000 men, women, and children were burned alive in the cave on a Sabbath day, a day upon which the Jews were commanded not to work

21. Judas had one military victory after another over the Syrians, as shown in Table 6-3, numbers 3-19. What was the only recorded defeat during this period and what two people were responsible? An attack by the Jews on the Gentiles of Jamnia (battle #15) by Joseph and Azariah

22. What is the only Jewish feast celebrated today that started during the inter-testament period? Hanukkah

23. When Antiochus IV Epiphanes was about to die, he sent a letter to the Jews. In it, he asked them to "*remember the public and private services rendered*" to them and to maintain their goodwill toward whom? To him and his son, Antiochus V

24. While Judas was besieging the Syrian Akra in Jerusalem, Antiochus V sent an enormous army to Jerusalem to stop the siege. This army included the equivalent of the modern-day tank. What was this weapon used by the Syrians? The elephant

25. After this battle of Beth-Zechariah, the besieger became the one besieged when Lysias blockaded Judas and the Jews in Jerusalem. Even though conquest was almost inevitable for the Jews, Lysias granted them free pardon and religious

liberty. Why? Lysias had to go back to Antioch to defeat Philip, the regent of Antiochus V

26. What evil man did Demetrius I install as high priest after Demetrius killed Lysias and Antiochus V Eupator? Alcimus

27. Of what bloodline was this priest installed by Demetrius I? Aaron's

28. With which Syrian military leader did Judas become friends? Nicanor

29. Before the battle of Elasa between Judas (Jews) and Bacchides (Syrians), Bacchides knew he had to keep Judas from fighting on Judas's terms. How did he do this? He terrorized the surrounding towns and forced Judas to come out and fight him

30. Which Syrian general finally managed to kill Judas? Bacchides

31. Who killed John (what family of the Nabataeans), the first son of Mattathias, in an apparent robbery of his baggage? The sons of Jambri

32. The death of John set off a series of back-and-forth skirmishes between the Maccabees and the Nabataeans. How did the Maccabees avenge their brother's death? They killed everyone in a wedding party of the family of Jambri

33. During the civil war in Syria between Demetrius I and Alexander Balas, both sides petitioned Jonathan for his support. Who won his support? Alexander Balas

34. Who was the only Syrian ruler with which the Maccabees did not have any war? Alexander Balas

35. What man proclaimed Antiochus VI Dionysus as king after the death of Alexander Balas and started a civil war with Demetrius II? Diodotus Tryphon

36. What event happened with Jonathan, as related to the armies of Demetrius II and Antiochus VI? All of Syria's soldiers became his allies

37. Tryphon, despite a peace treaty with Jonathan, needed Jonathan out of the way. Why? Because Tryphon wanted to kill Antiochus VI and knew that he would have a problem with the Jews (and Jonathan) if he did this before eliminating Jonathan

38. Tryphon tricked Jonathan into leaving the bulk of his army behind and going with him to Ptolemais. What happened to Jonathan and his men there? Tryphon captured him and killed his men

39. How many of Jonathan's men did Tryphon kill at Ptolemais? 1,000

40. Why did Simon comply with Tryphon's demand for 100 talents and two of Jonathan's sons as hostages in exchange for Jonathan? Because he knew that if he just ignored his terms and Tryphon killed Jonathan, then the people would blame him for doing nothing to get his brother back

41. Who was the last survivor of Mattathias's five sons? Simon

42. Simon re-established a peace treaty with Demetrius II, a former enemy. Why? Because they had a common enemy, Tryphon

43. When the Parthians captured Demetrius II, who became king of Syria? Antiochus VII Sidetes

44. What minor leader of the plain of Jericho killed Simon? Ptolemy, son of Abubus

45. What title did the people bestow upon Simon? Their leader and high priest forever

46. How many battles (out of 40 *total* among Mattathias, Judas, Jonathan, and Simon) were won by the Maccabees? Thirty-two

47. For how many treaties (out of 22 *total* among Judas, Jonathan, and Simon) was Jonathan responsible? Twelve

48. Which Syrian king made the most impressive/exhaustive list of promises to Jonathan that was ultimately refused by Jonathan? Demetrius I Soter

49. Did Tryphon intend to keep his promises made to Jonathan? No

50. What was the famous "day" in the summer of 168 BC that may have precipitated the Maccabean revolt? The "Day of Eleusis"

51. Why was the Maccabean revolt caused by these events (see the last question)? Because the Romans snatched Egypt from Antiochus IV Epiphanes's control, he vented his rage on the Jews, thus precipitating the revolt against his atrocities

52. What statement in I Maccabees 14:41 set the stage for the beginning of the Hasmonean dynasty? The Jews made Simon *"their leader and high priest forever"*

Chapter 7
▪ The Hasmonean Dynasty ▪

1. With whom did the Hasmonean period begin, according to most literature? Simon
2. Who else may have started the Hasmonean period (two men)? Jonathan or John Hyrcanus I
3. What defines the Hasmonean period and delineates it from the Maccabean period? A legitimization of the high priesthood in the Maccabean descendants
4. Which Hasmonean ruler killed his mother and (indirectly) a brother? Aristobulus I
5. According to Jewish tradition, high priests were supposed to be descendants of Aaron, the first high priest, and of the tribe of Levi. Who was the high priest during the Hasmonean period that was of the tribe of Benjamin? Menelaus
6. Who was the only Hasmonean ruler who was not also a high priest? Salome Alexandra
7. Which legitimate high priest fled to Egypt and established a temple there? Onias IV
8. Who removed Onias III from the high priesthood, and with whom was he replaced? Antiochus IV Epiphanes, Jason
9. About how long was it from the time Mattathias killed the Seleucid officials in Modein and the time the Jews had total independence under Judas? About 27 years
10. What things did John Hyrcanus I do to ensure hatred of the Samaritans toward the Jews? He destroyed their temple on Mt. Gerizim and destroyed the city of Samaria
11. Name one way in which John Hyrcanus I became an oppressor as opposed to a victim. He forced circumcision on all those he conquered
12. Around the time of John Hyrcanus I, the Pharisees and Sadducees are mentioned by name for the first time, and Hyrcanus switched from being a Pharisee to a Sadducee. Why did he switch? A member of the Pharisees accused Hyrcanus of being a Seleucid descendant
13. This switch of John Hyrcanus I to being a Sadducee fundamentally established the Sadducees as overseers of two

Jewish institutions. What were these institutions? The Temple
and the high priesthood

14. What Jewish establishment did the Pharisees come to oversee?
The synagogues

15. In a general sense, what philosophy did the Sadducees adopt?
Hellenization

16. In a general sense, what philosophy did the Pharisees adopt?
Orthodoxy/Hasidm

17. Name one reason John Hyrcanus I might have had significant
disagreements with his father or grandfather. John Hyrcanus
was forcing people to do things against their will, just as the
Seleucids had done to them

18. When John Hyrcanus died, he wanted the kingdom shared by
his wife and son, Aristobulus I. What did Aristobulus I do to
Hyrcanus's wife (and his mother)? Put her in prison and let
her starve to death

19. What did Aristobulus I do with his four brothers? Imprisoned
three and (indirectly) killed the fourth

20. The people of Ptolemais apparently were not very well liked.
What four leaders besieged the city on four separate
occasions? Alexander Jannaeus, Ptolemy IX Lathyros,
Cleopatra III, and Tigranes of Armenia

21. How many Jews (mostly Pharisees) were killed by Alexander
Jannaeus? About 50,000

22. Why was it odd that the Jews appealed to Demetrius III
Eucaerus for help against Alexander Jannaeus? They pleaded
to a descendant of the Seleucids for help against a descendant
of the Maccabees

23. The schism between the Pharisees and Sadducees became
significant during the time of Alexander Jannaeus because of
the way he treated the Pharisees. What good advice did the
otherwise sorry Jannaeus give his wife when he was on his
deathbed? Give the Pharisees some authority and give them
my body to do what they will

24. What appointment was made by Salome Alexandra for the
high priesthood, and why was it a precursor for trouble after
she died? She appointed her son, Hyrcanus II, to be high priest
who was a weak Pharisee, while her other son, Aristobulus II
was a strong Sadducee

25. During the civil wars between Aristobulus II and Hyrcanus II,
both sides appealed to the Roman General Pompey for

assistance. Whose side did Pompey (through his subordinate, Scaurus) initially take and why? Whose side did he ultimately take and why? First, he took the side of Aristobulus II because he offered him money. When Aristobulus did not do what he told him to, he took the side of Hyrcanus

26. What year was it when Pompey took Jerusalem and set Hyrcanus II up as a Roman puppet high priest? 63 BC

27. How did Aristobulus II die, after he was released from captivity by Julius Caesar in 49 BC? Pompey had him poisoned

28. A son of Aristobulus II is very hard to separate historically from Herod the Great. Who was he? Antigonus II

29. What did Antigonus II use as his bargaining chip with the Parthians to rid the kingdom of Hyrcanus II and Herod the Great? 1,000 talents and 500 women from principle Jewish families

30. When Herod the Great's life was in danger and he was fleeing from the Parthians, why did he build a monument at Herodium? Because he rebuffed a Jewish attack there

31. Why did Antigonus II cut off Hyrcanus II's ears? To disqualify him from being high priest

32. When Hyrcanus II and Phasael were taken captive by the Parthians, how did Phasael try to kill himself? By throwing himself down and hitting his head on a rock

33. When Herod finally made it to Rome and got an audience with Mark Antony and the Roman Senate, what did they do that surprised Herod? They made him king of the Jews instead of a blood-related Hasmonean

34. During Herod's campaign to subdue the regions of Judea and Samaria, there was one decisive battle against the forces of Antigonus II that broke *"the spirits of the enemy."* What commander of Antigonus was killed and had his head cut off? Pappus

35. Whom did Herod marry during his siege of Jerusalem, his new wife's hometown? Mariamne I

36. Why did Herod pay Antony a large sum of money to kill Antigonus II after the fall of Jerusalem? He was afraid Antigonus would convince the Roman Senate that he, or one of his heirs, should rightfully be king

37. What two people prodded Herod to make Aristobulus III, the son of Alexander II, the high priest? His wife Mariamne, who

was Aristobulus's brother, and his mother-in-law, Alexandra
(Mariamne's and Aristobulus's mother)

38. What man was high priest immediately before Aristobulus III
and immediately after Aristobulus III? Ananelus

39. Aristobulus III was 17 years old when Herod had him killed.
How did he die? A servant or servants of Herod drowned him

40. Why did Herod want Hyrcanus II to come back to Jerusalem
from Babylon? So he could eventually kill him

41. When Herod went to see Antony at the behest of Alexandra
and Cleopatra VII for the murder of Aristobulus III, what was
the "official" story of why Herod ordered Mariamne killed if
Antony killed him? What was the unofficial story? The
official story was that he loved her so much he could not bear
for her to be with another man. The unofficial story was that
he was not going to let Mark Antony have her if Antony killed
him.

42. Name all the Hasmoneans that were killed by Herod the Great.
Hyrcanus II, Aristobulus III, Antigonus II, Mariamne I,
Alexandra, Aristobulus IV, and Alexander

Chapter 8
▪ The Herodian Dynasty ▪

1. How many years did Herod the Great rule as king over the Jews? 37 years
2. Who were the parents of Herod the Great? Cypros I and Antipater II
3. Name the siblings of Herod the Great. Salome, Phasael I, Joseph and Pheroras
4. Who was the eldest child of Herod the Great? Antipater III
5. How many wives did Herod the Great have? Ten
6. Which of Herod's wives did not have children, as far as we know? His fourth and fifth wives
7. Who were the noteworthy sons of the Hasmonean princess, Mariamne I, and Herod the Great? Aristobulus IV and Alexander
8. Who were the notable sons of Malthace and Herod the Great? Herod Archelaus and Herod Antipas
9. Which "Philip" did Herodias marry? Herod Philip Boethus
10. Which "Philip" did Salome, the daughter of Herodias, marry? Philip the Tetrarch
11. The second wife of Herod the Great was Mariamne I, who was a Hasmonean. She was the daughter of whom (hint: go back to Chapter 7)? Alexander II and Alexandra
12. During what years was Herod the Great's father, Antipater II, procurator over Judea? 48-43 BC
13. What region did Herod the Great start out his career as governor? Galilee
14. When Herod the Great became king of the Jews, who was the Roman ruler at the time? Mark Antony
15. When Herod the Great was reconfirmed as the king of the Jews, who was the Roman emperor at the time? Octavian
16. When Mark Antony was preparing for war with Octavian at Actium (where Antony would be ultimately defeated), Herod offered to help Antony. Why did Antony refuse his help? Because Antony wanted Herod to "punish the king of Arabia."
17. When Octavian defeated Antony at Actium (and he finally committed suicide with Cleopatra VII), Herod's political career and life were in danger when Octavian took over the

Roman government. How did Herod defend himself to Octavian? He made no apologies to Octavian and told him to observe how he (Herod) treated his friends (in this case Antony) and that he would do the same for Octavian.

18. Name three of Herod's building projects. The Temple, the Temple Mount, the fortress at Masada

19. When Herod the Great knew he was getting ready to die, he commanded that a principle man from each Jewish family be locked up in the Hippodrome and killed upon his death. Why did he do this? He did this so that the whole nation would mourn his death greater than any king before him.

20. When Herod the Great took Alexander and Aristobulus IV to Rome to try them in front of Caesar Augustus (Octavian), who mounted a brilliant defense on behalf of the two brothers? Alexander

21. During the second trial of Alexander and Aristobulus IV before the Syrian governor Saturninus, Herod the Great did not let any witnesses testify and did not let the brothers defend themselves. On whose authority did Herod state that everything was true? His own

22. Which of Herod's sons had a verifiable conspiracy to kill Herod? Antipater III

23. Who was involved in this plot? Mariamne II (Herod's third wife), Pheroras (Herod's brother), Pheroras's wife, Antipater's mother Doris (Herod's first wife), Pheroras's wife's mother, Pheroras's wife's sister, and many others

24. How did Herod the Great find out about the conspiracy? After Pheroras had died, two of Pheroras's freedmen came to Herod accusing Pheroras's wife of killing him. Herod then tortured people to see if it was true and discovered the conspiracy against him.

25. Antipater III attempted to implicate two of Herod the Great's sons in his murder, even before it happened. Who were they? Herod Archelaus and Philip the (soon-to-be) Tetrarch

26. What sibling of Herod the Great was also falsely implicated in the plot to kill Herod the Great, discovered in forged letters with Acme, a servant of Caesar Augustus's wife, Julia? Salome

27. After Antipater III's imprisonment for his attempt to kill his father, what did he do that finally made Herod decide to kill him? He tried to bribe the jailor and promised him greatness

in the kingdom he would establish after Herod's death. The jailor then went to Herod and told him everything Antipater had said

28. When Herod the Great died, it looked as if Herod Archelaus would become the new king, as stated in Herod the Great's will. Who had to give final approval of this arrangement? Caesar Augustus (Octavian)

29. Who was in a previous will of Herod the Great as being the rightful heir to his throne? Herod Antipas

30. What three sons of Herod the Great got various portions of the kingdom? Archelaus, Antipas and Philip the (now) Tetrarch

31. Which son obtained rule over Judea (and Jerusalem)? Archelaus

32. When Herod the Great died and his kingdom was split among three of his children, which one was, arguably, the best ruler? Philip the Tetrarch

33. Which of the three siblings ruled the longest and when did he reign? Antipas from 4 BC to AD 39

34. Who was Herod Philip Boethus's wife that Herod Antipas "stole"? Herodias

35. Who condemned Antipas's marriage to Boethus's wife? John the Baptist

36. Who danced before Antipas that prompted him to give her whatever she wanted, and to whom was she related? Salome, the daughter of Herodias

37. For what did this woman ask? The head of John the Baptist on a platter

38. When Herod Antipas petitioned the new emperor of Rome, Caius (Caligula), to be king, what did Caius do? He banished him to Lyons, a city of Gaul, and gave all his money to Herod Agrippa I

39. Why did Herod the Great remove Herod Philip Boethus from his will? Because Boethus's mother, Mariamne II, was part of the plot to kill Herod the Great

40. How many Herods does the New Testament mention? Seven

41. Which two Roman emperors gave territory to Herod Agrippa I to rule? Caius (Caligula) and Claudius

42. When Herod Agrippa I ruled Judea as king, what were the titles of the Roman officials that ruled the territory before and after? Prefects and procurators

43. Who killed the father of Herod Agrippa I? Herod the Great, his grandfather
44. Why did Tiberius imprison Agrippa I? Because Agrippa had prayed that Tiberius would soon die and that his friend Caius (Caligula) would become emperor
45. What did Caius give Agrippa I after he released him from prison? A gold chain equal in weight to the iron one that bound him
46. What brother-in-law was Agrippa I responsible for having exiled? Herod Antipas
47. In general, how did Agrippa I treat the Jews, how did this compare to how he treated the Christians, and what two authors provide some of this information? He treated the Jews well but treated the Christians badly, as told by Josephus and Luke
48. Agrippa I got along well with most of the leaders of the various kingdoms and provinces, except one. Who was this? Gnaeus Vibius Marcus, governor of the Syrian province
49. What was a primary cause of the procurators taking over Judea after the reign of Herod Agrippa I? Because of the bad feelings that the governor of Syria (Marcus) and Herod Agrippa I had for each other, Claudius sent a procurator to Judea and a new governor to Syria after Agrippa's death.
50. What two Roman emperors granted Agrippa II territory? Claudius and Nero
51. How many years did Agrippa II continue to rule after the destruction of the Temple in Jerusalem? 22 years
52. Who was ruling Judea at the time of the destruction of the Temple? Marcus Antonius Julianus, a Roman procurator
53. In what year was the entire Temple complex completed, under whose reign was it completed, and how many years were taken to complete it? AD 64, Agrippa II, 84 years
54. What were the Roman titles (kings, procurators, etc.) of all the rulers over Judea from 37 BC to AD 70? What years were these rulers with these titles in effect? King (37 BC-4 BC), Ethnarch (4 BC-AD 6), Prefect (AD 6-AD 41), King (AD 41-AD 44), and Procurator (AD 44-AD 70)
55. What is the definition of an ethnarch? Ruler of an ethnic group
56. What is the definition of a tetrarch? Ruler of a fourth of a region

57. What was one reason Joseph and Mary did not return to Judea with Jesus? Because Herod Archelaus ruled Judea, and he was as evil as Herod the Great

58. Which Herod tried Jesus before his crucifixion? Herod Antipas

59. Which Herod executed the apostle James? Herod Agrippa I

60. Before which Herod did the apostle, Paul, make his defense? Herod Agrippa II

Chapter 9
▪ Roman Prefects, Procurators, Legates, and Governors ▪

1. What was the name of Caesarea before being rebuilt by Herod the Great? Strato's Tower
2. Over what three regions was Pontius Pilate prefect? Judea, Samaria, and Idumea
3. Going back to Figure 8-5, list the title of the rulers of Judea/Judaea from 37 BC to AD 70 and the period in which persons of this title reigned. King (37 BC – 4 BC), Ethnarch (4 BC – AD 6), Prefect (AD 6 – AD 41), King (AD 41 – AD 44), Procurator (AD 44 – AD 70)
4. How many prefects were there that ruled over Judaea, and what was the approximate total number of years they reigned? Seven, for about 35-36 years
5. How many procurators were there that ruled over Judaea and what was the approximate total number of years they reigned? Eight, for about 26-27 years
6. What king governed between the prefects and procurators and how many years did he reign? King Herod Agrippa I, for about three to four years
7. Into what two types of provinces was the Roman Empire divided? Imperial and Senatorial
8. Which type of province typically had a military presence? Imperial
9. What Roman province did Judaea fall under administratively? The Syrian Province
10. To whom did the prefects and procurators answer in their chain of command? The governor of the Syrian Province
11. What are the two names often given to the new province created by the Romans that encompassed Judea, Samaria, and Idumea? Judaea or Iudaea
12. List the prefects and the times they ruled. Coponius (AD 6 – 9), Marcus Ambivius (AD 9-12), Annius Rufus (AD 12-15), Valerius Gratus (AD 15-26), Pontius Pilate (AD 26-36), Marcellus (AD 36-37), and Marullus (AD 37-41)
13. List the procurators and the times they ruled. Cuspius Fadus (AD 44-46), Tiberius Alexander (AD 46-48), Ventidius

Cumanus (AD 48-52), Marcus Antonius Felix (AD 52-60), Porcius Festus (AD 60-62), Lucceius Albinus (AD 62-64), Gessius Florus (AD 64-66), and Marcus Antonius Julianus (AD 66-70)

14. Where did the prefects and procurators make their home? Caesarea

15. Where did the Syrian governors make their home? Antioch

16. Using Figure 9-2 as a guide, to which Syrian governors did Pontius Pilate answer (and for what years) and under which emperor did these governors rule? He answered to Lucius Aelius Lamia from 26-32, Lucius Pomponius Flaccus from AD 32-35 and Lucius Vitellius from AD 35-36. All of these governors ruled under Emperor Tiberius

17. How many high priests did the prefect Valerius Gratus appoint? Four

18. Annas I was the father of how many other high priests? Five

19. List two examples of how Pilate antagonized the Jews. He brought images of Tiberius into Jerusalem, and he set up gold shields in Herod's Palace

20. Under which prefect did the first Christian martyrdom happen, and who was the martyr? Marcellus, Stephen

21. Why did Emperor Claudius not just add Judaea to the Syrian province after the death of Herod Agrippa I, but chose to put it under a procurator instead? Because the current Syrian governor at the time, Gnaeus Marcus, and Herod Agrippa I did not get along, and Claudius did not give Marcus the territory out of respect for Agrippa

22. In what capacity did the second procurator of Judaea, Tiberius Alexander, serve at the destruction of Jerusalem? Second in command to Titus

23. How did Ventidius Cumanus punish the soldier that tore up the Law of Moses in one of the villages outside Jerusalem? He had him beheaded

24. Who were the two historically named people to die in the eruption of Mount Vesuvius in AD 79? Marcus Antonius Agrippa (son of Felix and Drusilla) and Pliny, the Elder

25. Before what two Roman procurators was the apostle Paul tried? Felix and Festus

26. Why did Festus want King Agrippa II to hear the case of Paul? Because Festus did not know what to write to Nero regarding the crimes of which Paul was allegedly guilty

27. Who was the only procurator to die in office? Festus
28. What Roman procurator was furious that James, the brother of Jesus, was stoned without his permission? Albinus
29. What group of people was in prison by the end of the reign of Albinus? Those who were not guilty of a serious crime but did not pay Albinus a bribe to get out
30. What one person, more than anyone else, was responsible for the Jews going to war with the Romans? The procurator, Gessius Florus
31. Why did this person want the Jews to go to war with the Romans? So his crimes against the Jews would not be brought to Rome's attention
32. What sister of Herod Agrippa II petitioned Florus to stop killing and looting the Jews? Berenice
33. Who was almost able to convince the Jews that going to war with Rome would be for naught? Agrippa II
34. What Roman governor of the Syrian province stood up to the Roman emperor Caligula (Caius) and refused to kill more than 10,000 Jews? Publius Petronius
35. Civil war broke out between the Jews before the war began with the Romans. What were the two fundamental desires of the Jews pitted against each other in this civil war? Those who wanted to go to war with Rome and those who opposed it
36. Name two cities (of at least four) where the Jews were wiped out by the other inhabitants during the reign of Gessius Florus. Caesarea and Alexandria (also Ptolemais and Damascus)
37. What famous man was the leader of the Jews in Galilee? Josephus, the Jewish historian
38. What three Roman legates ruled Judaea from after Jerusalem's destruction until AD 81? Sextus Vettulenus Cerialis (70-71), Lucilius Bassus (71-72), and Lucius Flavius Silva (72-81)
39. Which Roman legate was responsible for taking the fortresses of Machaerus and Herodium? Lucilius Bassus
40. Which Roman legate was famous for his siege and capture of the last zealot holdout on Masada? Lucius Flavius Silva
41. Which two Syrian governors likely governed twice? Gaius Cassius Longinus (#6 and #14) and Publius Sulpicius Quirinius (#28 and #31)
42. What Syrian governor sent Pontius Pilate to Emperor Tiberius to answer for his crimes against the Samaritans? Lucius Vitellius

43. When Publius Petronius was ordered to attack the Jews because of their unwillingness to put a statue of Caligula in the Temple, what did he do? He let the Jews return to their homes and told them he would deal with the emperor

Chapter 10
▪ The Roman Conquest of Galilee, Jerusalem, and Masada ▪

1. What great general was sent by Nero to Galilee to put an end to the Jewish uprising? Vespasian
2. What was the name of the city where the male inhabitants were killed between the city's double walls? Japha
3. In what city did the Romans finally capture Josephus? Jotapata
4. How many other men did the Romans seize with Josephus at the time and why? One other who, along with Josephus, were the last two to survive after the others had cast lots and killed each other
5. After Josephus was caught and brought before Vespasian, what did Josephus tell Vespasian and his son Titus that kept them from sending him to Nero? He told them that they would both be emperors one day
6. What other prediction, verified by one of his compatriots, had Josephus made? That Jotapata would fall to the Romans in 47 days
7. During Vespasian's preparation to besiege Jerusalem, what news made him stop? That Nero had died
8. Who were the four emperors that made up "the year of four emperors"? Galba, Otho, Vitellius, and Vespasian
9. There were three factions of zealots fighting in the civil war among the Jews in Jerusalem. Who were the three leaders of these factions? Eleazar, the son of Simon; Simon, the son of Gioras; and John, the son of Levi
10. Who was the Roman ambassador to the Jews during the siege of Jerusalem? Josephus
11. Why was the siege of Jerusalem personal to Josephus? Because many of his family were in Jerusalem, including his mother and wife
12. Which part of Jerusalem was the first to fall to the Romans and in which they then set up their camp? The "New City"
13. When Titus's plan to take the Antonia Fortress and his breach of the last wall (known as the first wall) failed, what did he

    then have built around the Jewish-controlled part of the city?
A siege wall

14. What did many of the Jews sneak out of Jerusalem when they were able to surrender to the Romans and how did they get it out? They swallowed gold pieces

15. What did Titus promise the zealots if they would only change the place in which they had chosen to fight? That the Romans would not destroy nor defile the Temple

16. When the Romans finally finished taking Jerusalem, what areas did they not even attempt to pillage? The houses where there were piles of dead rotting bodies

17. What were the only parts of Jerusalem that Titus did not destroy? The western wall of the Temple mount and Herod's three towers

18. How many of the "tallest and most beautiful" of the young Jews taken captive were sent to Rome for the triumph there? 700

19. Many of the Jews were either sold as slaves or given to the various Roman provinces as presents. For what purpose were these presents? For participation in the gladiatorial games

20. On what other occasion had Jerusalem been destroyed before its destruction in AD 70? Nebuchadnezzar destroyed it in 587 BC

21. Who was the leader of the zealots at Masada? Eleazar ben Ya'ir

22. Name two reasons Herod the Great enhanced and provisioned Masada as much as he did. In case the Jews revolted against him or if Cleopatra had convinced Mark Antony to kill him and take Judea for her sake

23. Who was the commander of the Roman forces besieging Masada? Flavius Silva

24. How did the last ten Jewish men die at Masada? The one who drew the "winning" lot killed the other nine and then killed himself

25. How many Jews died at Masada and how many lived? 960 (or 953) and 7

26. What was inscribed on one of the ostraca found at Masada in the early 1960s, and to whom does this probably refer? "Ben Ya'ir," the leader of the zealots at Masada (Eleazar)

27. Who ordered the Jewish temple in Egypt destroyed? Vespasian

28. What were three monuments built by the Romans to signify their victory over the Jews? The Temple of Peace (Forum of Vespasian), the Flavian Amphitheater, and the Arch of Titus

Chapter 11
▪ Roman History and Government ▪

1. Roman history may be divided into what three parts? The monarchy, the Republic, and the Empire
2. How many kings ruled during the monarchy? Seven
3. During the Roman Republic, how many consuls typically were there at a given time? Two (co-consuls)
4. With whom did Rome fight the Punic Wars? Carthage
5. When the Roman Empire divided into a western and eastern half, what was the capital of each territory? Rome (west) and Constantinople (east)
6. What was the defining event that began the Roman Empire, at least as far as we have defined it in this book? When the Senate declared Octavian to be Augustus
7. What is the name of the period, which followed the collapse of the Western Roman Empire? The Middle Ages (or Medieval Period)
8. What social class of Roman citizens were typically large landowners and controlled Roman politics and religion? Patricians
9. Who were the ordinary Roman citizens? Plebeians
10. What is the name of the power some magistrates had that allowed them to interpret and carry out the law, impose the death penalty, and have the ultimate authority over others? Imperium
11. Approximately how many total dictators were there during the Republic, and who were two of the most famous ones? 90, Julius Caesar and Lucius Sulla
12. What was the typical length of time a dictator held office? Six months
13. What was the name of the office that was second in command to a dictator? Master of the Horse
14. How many senators were there during the monarchy, during the time of Julius Caesar, and during the time of Caesar Augustus? 100, 900, 600
15. What office represented the Plebeians, could veto any magistrate's legislative decision (except those of dictators), and could call a Senate assembly? Tribune of the Plebs

16. Who served the most terms as consul during the Republic? Gaius Marius
17. Who was probably the richest man in Roman history? Marcus Crassus
18. Who was the first "dictator for life" that stepped down before he died? Lucius Sulla
19. Who was the first "dictator for life" that held the title until he died? Julius Caesar
20. Which three men formed the First Triumvirate? Julius Caesar, Marcus Crassus, and Gnaeus Pompey
21. Which three men formed the Second Triumvirate? Mark Antony, Marcus Lepidus, and Gaius Octavius
22. What was the process called (made famous predominantly during the time of Gaius Marius and Lucius Sulla) whereby these men could eliminate their political enemies by killing them and taking their property? Proscription
23. Who was the young, future Roman leader on Sulla's list of proscriptions that Sulla ultimately removed from his list? Julius Caesar
24. What was one of the primary reasons Marcus Crassus disliked Gnaeus Pompey? Because Pompey undeservedly took much of the credit for defeating the uprising by Spartacus and his army of slaves and gladiators
25. What Roman general and proconsul subdued Jerusalem and added Judea to the Roman province of Syria in 63 BC? Pompey
26. What two events caused the First Triumvirate to collapse? The death of Caesar's daughter and Pompey's wife, Julia, and the death of Crassus the following year
27. What did Pompey, as consul, demand of Caesar before he would allow him to run as consul? That Caesar disband his army
28. What river in northeastern Italy did Caesar cross to begin the civil war with Pompey? The Rubicon River
29. At the end of the civil war between Caesar and Pompey, who ordered Pompey killed and his head presented to Caesar? The Egyptian king, Ptolemy XIII
30. What rival of the person that had Pompey killed became a consort to Julius Caesar? Cleopatra VII
31. How many days had to be inserted in the Roman calendar to synchronize with the newly formed Julian calendar? Eighty

32. On what date did about 60 senators kill Julius Caesar? March 15, 44 BC
33. Who did Caesar declare in his will to be his heir? Octavian, his adopted son
34. As ruler of the eastern provinces during the Second Triumvirate, whom did Antony summon to see him that would later become his wife? Cleopatra VII
35. Name two things Octavian used against Antony to discredit him with the Roman people. That he left his pregnant wife to be with Cleopatra VII and that Antony had given Roman lands to Cleopatra's children
36. On whom did the Senate declare war in 32 BC, at the behest of Octavian? Cleopatra VII
37. After Antony and Cleopatra had committed suicide, whom did Octavian kill? Julius Caesar and Cleopatra's son, Caesarion
38. Who was the first Roman emperor? Octavian (Augustus)
39. What four people did Caesar Augustus adopt? Tiberius, Agrippa Posthumus, Lucius Caesar, and Gaius Caesar
40. Why was Caesar Augustus known as the "son of a god"? Because his adoptive father, Julius Caesar, had been deified by the Roman Senate after his death
41. What Roman month did the Senate rename to August in honor of Augustus? Sextilis
42. How many terms did Octavian/Augustus serve as consul, including those during the Empire period? Thirteen
43. Who was the second emperor and how was he related to Augustus? Tiberius was Augustus's stepson and adopted son
44. How did Rome's second emperor leave the decision to the gods as to whom the next emperor would be after he died? Whoever came in to see him first the next morning was the one to be emperor
45. In what two ways was Caligula related to Tiberius? He was Tiberius's great nephew (Germanicus's son) as well as his step daughter's (Agrippina the Elder) son
46. Who was the chief conspirator in the death of Caligula? Cherea
47. How was Claudius, the fourth Roman emperor, related to Caesar Augustus? He was his step grandson
48. How was Claudius related to Mark Antony? He was his grandson

49. After the assassination of Caligula, the Roman Empire almost reverted to the Republic form of government. What group of influential people decided they wanted to maintain a sole ruler and thus the Empire form of government? The military
50. Who was put to death by Claudius in spite of the "work he had done was a glorious one?" Cherea
51. Who was rewarded by Claudius with a kingdom essentially the same size as that of Herod the Great? Agrippa I
52. Whom did Claudius adopt that became the fifth Roman emperor? Nero
53. How many times did Nero marry and how many of them were women? Four and three
54. Name three of Nero's relatives he had killed. His mother and two of his wives
55. Nero was an aggressive persecutor of Christians. Name one way he had Christians killed. He had them covered in pitch, impaled them on a stake and set them on fire
56. What apostle appealed his case to the Roman emperor, Nero? Paul
57. Who were the four emperors associated with the "year of the four emperors?" Galba, Otho, Vitellius and Vespasian
58. Who of these four emperors might have made a good leader if he had not killed himself after ruling for only three months? Otho
59. What was the name of the dynasty that the ninth emperor, Vespasian, formed? The Flavian dynasty
60. What two sons of Vespasian became emperors? Titus and Domitian
61. Who was the first emperor to be the blood-relative son of a previous emperor? Titus
62. What were Vespasian's dying words? "Dear me! I must be turning into a god."

Chapter 12
▪ Jewish Politics, Holidays, and Institutions ▪

1. Which of the seven sects discussed in this chapter does the New Testament not mention? The Essenes
2. Which four sects had their beginning during the time of the Hasmoneans? The Sadducees, Pharisees, Essenes, and Herodians
3. What one critical event during the time of Simon Maccabeus gave rise to the Sadducees? When Simon became high priest, replacing the descendants from the line of Aaron
4. Between which two sons of Salome Alexandra was one of the first major conflicts between Pharisees and Sadducees? Hyrcanus II and Aristobulus II
5. What did Cyrus the Great *not* allow the Jews to have when they returned from Babylonian captivity that caused the priesthood to become so powerful? A king
6. Why did the Sadducees not believe in Jesus as the Messiah? They did not believe in the idea of a messiah
7. Name three beliefs (or non-beliefs) of the Sadducees. They did not believe in angels, spirits, or immortality
8. What two institutions did the Sadducees dominate? The Temple and the Sanhedrin
9. Name three beliefs of the Pharisees. Physical resurrection, angels, and the Messiah
10. Explain how Sadducees and Pharisees might explain compensation regarding "an eye for an eye." The Sadducees might interpret it literally, requiring the eye be put out of the offender, whereas the Pharisees might demand the value of the eye paid as restitution
11. What was the additional set of laws (in addition to *the* law) with which the Pharisees required compliance? The oral law
12. What were the two leading schools of philosophy to which Pharisees typically subscribed? The school of Shammai and the school of Hillel
13. Which of these two schools was probably the most antagonistic toward Jesus? The school of Shammai
14. Name three prominent Pharisees that we read about in the New Testament. Paul, Joseph of Arimathea, and Gamaliel

15. What did Paul say to the Sanhedrin (as told in Acts 22:30-23:10) that had the council at each other's throats? He said he was a Pharisee and the son of a Pharisee
16. What sect could be considered the militant wing of the Pharisees? The zealots
17. What apostle of Jesus was almost certainly a zealot? Simon Zealotes
18. What was one of the primary goals of the zealots? To drive Rome out of Judaea
19. Name three beliefs of the Essenes. All matter was evil, they rejected Temple worship, they believed in spiritual immortality but not a bodily resurrection
20. What is the only book of the Bible not found, in part or whole, in the Dead Sea Scrolls? Esther
21. Why did the Essenes not believe in Jesus as the Messiah? Because they believed all matter is evil, including all flesh and blood
22. Blasphemy of what man was a capital offense to the Essenes? Moses
23. With whom were the Herodians in cahoots when they confronted Jesus on two occasions? The Pharisees
24. Did the Herodians philosophically lean more toward the Pharisees or the Sadducees? The Sadducees
25. How did publicans typically make their living? By collecting and keeping more than the taxes that were owed to the Romans
26. What two publicans does the New Testament mention? Matthew, the apostle, and Zacchaeus, a tax collector in Jericho
27. Besides the Pharisees, what group was typically considered a religious authority? The scribes
28. Who were the interpreters of the law? The scribes
29. What time of day do Jewish holidays start? Sunset the day before
30. When does Yom Kippur start (the Jewish month and day) and what range of Gregorian dates can this be? 10 Tishri, anywhere from September 14 to October 14
31. What was the first mandated Jewish holiday in the Old Testament? The Sabbath
32. What Jewish holiday supersedes Rosh Chodesh Tishri? Rosh Hashanah
33. What two Jewish holidays collectively are referred to as "High Holy Days"? Rosh Hashanah and Yom Kippur

34. What is the holiest day of the year for Jews? Yom Kippur
35. What holiday commemorates the years the Jews spent wandering in the desert on their way to the Promised Land? Sukkot or the Feast of Tabernacles
36. What does Hanukkah celebrate? The defeat of Antiochus Epiphanes and the re-dedication of the Temple
37. What holiday celebrates the defeat of Haman? Purim
38. What does Passover commemorate? The Jews' release from Egyptian slavery and the sparing of their firstborn children
39. What is the only Jewish holiday with its origin in the inter-testament period? Hanukkah
40. What does the unleavened bread commemorate during the Passover feast? The Jews left Egypt so quickly that the bread did not have time to rise
41. What is the ritual meal called that is eaten during the Passover holiday? Seder
42. What day started the "counting of the Omer"? The second day of Passover, also known as the Feast of Firstfruits
43. What day follows the last day of the "counting of the Omer"? Pentecost or Shavuot
44. What holiday is known as the saddest day in Jewish history and why is it the most tragic day? Tisha B'Av, because both Temples were destroyed on this date, 656 years apart
45. What day and month on the Jewish calendar was May 14, 1948, and why was this day significant? 5 Iyar, the day of the founding of the Jewish state of Israel
46. With what event does the history of the Temple Mount begin? Where Abraham brought Isaac for sacrifice
47. How many different Temple Mounts were there? Three
48. What two features can we see today that likely denote where "Solomon's" Temple Mount once was? The "bend" in the eastern wall and the "step" on the northwest corner leading up to the Muslim platform
49. What feature can we see today that likely denotes where the Hasmonean Temple Mount once was? The "seam" in the eastern wall
50. How many fortresses were there on the Temple Mount throughout history? Seven
51. How many fortresses were there on the northwest corner of the Solomon-era Temple Mount throughout history? Five

52. From about 960 BC to AD 70, not counting construction periods, when was there not a Temple? From about 587 BC to about 515 BC
53. What two Temples are typically called the second Temple in most of the literature? Zerubbabel's and Herod's Temples
54. What is the primary structure standing on the Temple Mount today where the second Temple likely stood? The Muslim Dome of the Rock
55. In what year was Herod's Temple completed, and when was it destroyed? AD 64, AD 70
56. What two rooms had the same sizes in all three Temples? The Holy Place and the Most Holy Place
57. What day was the high priest allowed to enter the Holy of Holies? Yom Kippur
58. What were the two pillars named that were outside Solomon's Temple? Jachin and Boaz
59. How many changes of clothes did the high priest use during Yom Kippur ceremonies? Five
60. How many tables of showbread and lamp stands were in Solomon's Temple? Ten of each
61. What animal's likeness was used to support the Molten Sea outside Solomon's Temple? How many were there? Oxen, 12
62. What items of furniture were in the Holy of Holies in Herod's Temple? None
63. How many acres was the Temple Mount when Herod completed building it? 35 acres ($141,640 \ m^2$)
64. Regarding Herod's Temple, what separated the Court of the Gentiles from the Sacred Enclosure, where no Gentiles were allowed? The *soreg*
65. What gate separated the Woman's Court from the Court of the Israelites? The Nicanor Gate
66. What animal's likeness was used to support the Laver outside Herod's Temple and how many were there? Lions, 12
67. What is the longest dimension of Herod's Temple Mount (the west side)? 1590 feet (485 m)
68. How many steps led up to the Nicanor Gate? 15
69. What precipitated the creation of the Jewish synagogues? When the Babylonians destroyed the Temple and displaced the Jews to Babylon, they needed a place to worship
70. What was the Great Sanhedrin? The Jewish high court

71. During what period was the Sanhedrin first mentioned?
During the reign of the Hasmonean, Alexander Janneaus

72. How many judges comprised the Great Sanhedrin? 71

73. How many judges comprised the smaller Sanhedrins? 23

74. At what point in time might the Sanhedrin no longer have been allowed to carry out capital punishment (thus requiring them to go to Pontius Pilate to get a death warrant)? Around AD 30

75. What could all male descendants of Aaron become? Priests

76. What did all male descendants of Levi become? Levites

77. Whose descendants did the line of high priests pass from after Uzzi was high priest? Ithamar

78. Through whom was Aaron the grandson of Levi? Jochebed

79. Through whom was Aaron the great grandson of Levi? Amram

80. How many animals were sacrificed at the dedication of Solomon's Temple and how many at the dedication of Zerubbabel's Temple? 142,000 and 712

81. Around what year was Solomon's Temple completed and what year was it destroyed? 960 and 587 BC

82. About what year was Zerubbabel's Temple completed? 515 BC

83. How many years was Herod's Temple complete before being destroyed by the Romans? About 6

Chapter 13
▪ Writings of the Inter-Testament Period ▪

1. In what language was the Septuagint written? Greek
2. Which Egyptian ruler probably commissioned the writing of the Septuagint? Ptolemy II Philadelphus
3. When was the Septuagint probably written? Between 284 and 247 BC
4. What was the name of Origen's work that laid out six different versions of the Bible in one volume? The Hexapla
5. What does the Greek word apocrypha mean and who coined the term? "Hidden" or "secret," devised by Jerome
6. How many apocryphal books are considered canonical by Roman Catholics? How many of those show up as additional books in the table of contents of their Bibles? Twelve and seven
7. What is the longest apocryphal book? Ecclesiasticus
8. How many apocryphal books are there in total, at least according to this book? Eighteen
9. What three apocryphal books sometimes are grouped into one book called the Additions to Daniel? The Prayer of Azariah and the Song of the Three Jews, Susanna, and Bel and the Dragon
10. Which apocryphal book sometimes becomes Chapter 6 of Baruch? The Letter of Jeremiah
11. Catholic Bibles do not include the apocryphal book of I Esdras; however, some Catholic Bibles have I Esdras in them. How is this possible? Because sometimes I Esdras is the same name used for Ezra
12. What other three names is the apocryphal book of II Esdras sometimes called? IV, V, and VI Esdras
13. Which one of the apocryphal books is not accepted by any major religious group as canonical? IV Maccabees
14. Russian Orthodox churches accept which apocryphal book as canonical (but no others accept)? II Esdras
15. In which apocryphal book is the Catholic doctrine of purgatory based? II Maccabees

16. Which were the three apocryphal books not in the original King James Version of 1611? III and IV Maccabees and Psalm 151

17. In the apocryphal book of Tobit, who was willing to marry Sarah, even though her first seven husbands died? Tobias, Tobit's son

18. For whom did Sarah's father have a grave dug? Tobias

19. In the book of Judith, of what ancient kingdom is Nebuchadnezzar stated incorrectly as king? Assyria

20. Whose head did Judith cut off? Holofernes, the general of Nebuchadnezzar

21. Why did Esther almost faint when she approached King Ahasuerus? Because he "*looked at her in fierce anger*," and she knew he could have her executed for just approaching him without being summoned

22. What is the only apocryphal book whose author is known by his actual name and what is his name? Ecclesiasticus, written by Jesus, the son of Sirach

23. What apocryphal book sarcastically talks about the utter uselessness of idols? The Letter of Jeremiah

24. What book is often combined with the book of Baruch to form its sixth chapter? The Letter of Jeremiah

25. What were the Hebrew names of Shadrack, Meshack, and Abednego? Hananiah, Mishael, and Azariah

26. Which book is considered one of the first detective stories or courtroom dramas? Susanna

27. In what lie did Daniel catch the two elders when they accused Susanna of adultery? They did not agree on what kind of tree that they saw Susanna under as she was committing adultery

28. In Bel and the Dragon, what prophet did an angel grab by the hair and transport from his home to Babylon to feed Daniel in the lion's den? Habakkuk

29. What book gives details on the battles of the Maccabee brothers and considered by most to be a reliable and valuable book? I Maccabees

30. What book is a condensed account of an earlier work by Jason of Cyrene? II Maccabees

31. In the only material that is unique to I Esdras (and is not found elsewhere in II Chronicles, Nehemiah, or Ezra), what one thing was found to be "strongest"? Women

32. In what *order* do the three parts (known as IV, V, and VI Esdras) appear in II Esdras? V, IV, and VI

33. Why is the name of III Maccabees a misnomer? It deals with events in the Ptolemaic period and has nothing to do with the Maccabees or the Seleucid period of Judea's history

34. As told in III Maccabees, how was Ptolemy IV Philopater going to have the Jews killed in the Hippodrome? He was going to have them trampled to death by drugged elephants

35. In IV Maccabees, what old scribe was tortured and put to death by Antiochus IV Epiphanes and his men? Eleazar

36. In what book do we read about the repentance of an evil king of Judah while he was captive in Babylon? The Prayer of Manasseh

37. What is the shortest apocryphal book, with just seven verses? Psalm 151

38. What does the word "Pseudepigrapha" mean? "False name" or "false inscription"

39. What sets pseudepigraphical books apart from other religious writings? In other words, what claim is made by each of their authors? That they are well-known biblical figures

40. From what pseudepigraphical book does Jude (in the biblical book of Jude) quote? I Enoch

41. To what other pseudepigraphical book does Jude possibly allude? The Assumption of Moses

42. To the Pharisees, to what did the oral law have the same standing? The written law

43. The oral law was eventually committed to writing and was known as what? The Mishnah

44. When was the oral law written down? Between AD 200 and 220

45. Unlike the written law of the Hebrew Bible (the Tanakh), how is the Mishnah laid out? By topic

46. The Mishnah strives to answer questions not addressed in the Hebrew Scriptures. What are the six major sections of the Mishnah? Agriculture, set feasts, women, damages, hallowed things, and purities

47. What is the name of the commentary on the Mishnah? The Gemara

48. What is the name of the document that encompasses both the oral law (Mishnah) and its commentary? The Talmud

49. Which version of the Talmud is the more authoritative and is the larger of the two? The Babylonian version
50. Christians typically study the Bible. What book do Jews commonly learn? The Talmud
51. What is the Jewish name for the Hebrew Bible? The Tanakh
52. What three components comprise the Hebrew Bible composed? The Torah, Nevi'im, and Ketuvim
53. How many books are in the Hebrew Bible? 24
54. What book in the Tanakh combines the twelve Minor Prophets? Trey Asar
55. In the most limited sense of the word, what is the Torah? The first five books of the Hebrew Bible
56. What is the Greek work for the first five books of the Hebrew Bible? Pentateuch
57. Sometimes the word Torah is a stand in for the entire Tanakh. What is the broadest use of the word Torah? In other words, what documents are included in this comprehensive definition of the Torah? The Tanakh and the Mishnah
58. What are the Targumim? Paraphrases, translations, free renderings and interpretations of Hebrew Scriptures into Aramaic
59. What words of Jesus on the cross were a mixture of Aramaic and Hebrew, at least as recorded by Matthew? "*Eli, Eli, lama sabachthani*"
60. Which part of this saying was in Aramaic? "*lama sabachthani*"
61. What are the Midrashim? Synagogue sermons
62. In one Midrash, whom did the young Abraham initially blame for smashing all the idols in his father's shop? The largest idol
63. According to another Midrash, who was Adam's first wife? Lilith

Chapter 14
▪ Money and Weights ▪

1. What six characteristics must money possess, according to the Federal Reserve Bank of St. Louis? (1) It must be durable, (2) It must be portable, (3) It must be divisible, (4) It must have a limited supply, (5) It must be acceptable, and (6) It must be uniform

2. Upon what system are our units of time (60 seconds per minute, 60 minutes per hour) based? The Babylonian sexagesimal system

3. Who probably introduced the Jews to coinage with their gold daric and silver siglos? The Persians

4. Which Syrian leader gave Simon Maccabeus the right to mint coins, even though Simon probably never did? Antiochus VII Sidetes

5. What type of coin was typically minted by local mints given that the imperial mints typically minted gold and silver coins? Bronze

6. What was the base unit of Jewish money (and still is today)? The shekel

7. What was the most widely coined and used silver shekel from the end of the inter-testament period through the New Testament period? The Tyrian shekel

8. What form of payment (coin) was required for the annual Temple tax? The Tyrian shekel

9. The term "widow's mite" did not exist in ancient times, but it was coined during the translation of Tyndale's New Testament. What Jewish coin was likely this "widow's mite"? The Lepton

10. What Jewish coin was worth two lepta? A prutah

11. How many shekels was a talent worth by the time of the New Testament? 3,000 shekels

12. What was the base unit of Greek money? The drachm

13. What was the base unit of Roman money? The denarius

14. What denomination of Jewish coin was about equal to the Roman quadrans? The prutah

15. What base-unit coin was about equal to the Roman denarius? The Greek drachm

16. What Roman coin was approximately equal to a day's wage for an unskilled worker? The denarius
17. What Roman gold coin was equal to 25 denarii? The aureus
18. In what period of history were the first Jewish coins minted? The Hasmonean period
19. Given the *very general assumptions* in this chapter, how much was the "widow's mite" (or Jewish lepton) worth in today's money (2016)? About $0.36
20. Given the same assumptions, how much was the Roman denarius worth? About $43.50
21. Given the same assumptions, how much was the Jewish talent worth? About $435,000
22. Approximately how many minutes of the labor of an unskilled worker was equivalent to a lepton? About 3 minutes
23. During the Roman period, how many prutot were there in a shekel? 256
24. How many shekels were in a talent by the end of the Babylonian captivity? 3,000
25. How many standards of Greek money were there? 16
26. What Greek coin was approximately equal to the Jewish shekel? The tetradrachm
27. What Roman coin was translated as a farthing in the King James Version? The quadrans
28. What base metals make up a brass coin? Copper and zinc
29. What base metals make up a bronze coin? Copper and tin (and possibly other metals)
30. How much could a person expect to make looking after a sick man? 2 denarii
31. What expensive vegetable might have cost a denarius? A cucumber
32. Besides Tyre, in what city might have Tyrian shekels been minted? Jerusalem
33. What was the name of the fee charged by the moneychangers, which was in addition to the half-shekel Temple tax? The *kolbon*
34. This fee might have been how many prutot (what range of values)? 5.3 to 12.8 prutot
35. At the time the King James Version was written, what Roman coin was the same value as the British silver penny? The denarius

36. In all the different English translations of Matthew 18:28 that discusses the "hundred denarii" (NRSV), give an example of the smallest translated value and another example of the largest (this could have different answers for each)? "Some tiny sum" to "a few thousand dollars"

37. What coin (x30) was likely used to pay Judas for betraying Jesus? The Tyrian shekel

38. What coin is likely the "tribute money" discussed in Matthew 22:17-22? The denarius

39. Of the rulers of Judea/Judaea, how many of them had their image or that of Caesar put on their coins for circulation in Judea/Judaea? None

40. Who was the only Roman prefect over Judaea to put a pagan religious symbol on one of his coins? Pontius Pilate

41. Of the Hasmonean rulers, who minted the most commonly found bronze prutot coins? Alexander Jannaeus

42. How many different coin designs did Herod the Great mint? At least 23

43. What did the Judaea Capta coins celebrate and commemorate? The destruction of Jerusalem and the overthrow of the Jews

Chapter 15
▪ Life in the Ancient World ▪

1. Why was Hezekiah's tunnel built? Because of the impending invasion by King Sennacherib of the Assyrians
2. During the time of Hezekiah, why were the people willing to sacrifice their houses? To build the Broad Wall for protection of the city
3. What separates Jerusalem from the Judean desert? The Mount of Olives
4. How far below the city streets did the Israelis find the remains of the *Burnt House*? About 20 feet
5. What happened to the extra meat from an animal sacrificed to a god and not eaten by the one making the sacrifice (or his family)? They sold it in the market
6. What four works (two by Homer and two by Hesiod) describe many of the Greek gods? The *Iliad* and *Odyssey* by Homer; and *Theogony* and *Works and Days* by Hesiod
7. What are the four major groups of the Greek gods and their offspring? (1) Primordial deities, (2) The Titans, (3) The Olympians, (4) The Heroes
8. Who was the original Greek god from which all the others came, including Gaia (The Earth)? Chaos, the Void
9. How many of the twelve Titans were male? Six
10. From where did Zeus and the other Olympians rule the world? From Mount Olympus in Greece
11. Name three events in the life of Alexander the Great that led him to believe he was the son of Zeus. When the priest of the temple of Amon-Ra in Egypt (Zeus Ammon) told him he was the son of the god; when the Persians bowed down to him as their new leader; when Olympia claimed Zeus impregnated her
12. What war is described by the events in Homer's *Iliad*? The Trojan War
13. Name the twelve Roman gods of the *Dii Concentes*. Juno, Vesta, Minerva, Ceres, Diana, and Venus, Mars, Mercury, Jupiter, Neptune, Vulcan, and Apollo
14. What was the name of the Roman god whose temple had the doors open during times of war and closed during times of peace? Janus

15. Which Roman god had a planet and an element named after him? Mercury
16. Which full-time priestesses served the goddess Vesta? The Vestal Virgins
17. What was the title of the "high priest of the Roman state" assumed by the Emperor, Augustus? Pontifex Maximus
18. What was the *divine spirit* of Emperor Augustus called, which he said should be worshiped instead of his person? His *genius*
19. What was one reason Romans could accept other religious beliefs into their system but had more trouble accommodating Judaism and Christianity? Because Judaism and Christianity were monotheistic
20. Which Greek god did the people of Lystra believe the apostle Paul to be? Hermes
21. Why was eating meat sacrificed to idols such a problem to early Christians? Because so much of it was in the markets
22. What was often the fate of Roman children, particularly girls, who were born weak, diseased, or otherwise unwanted by the Roman father? They might be left on a trash heap to die and then might be taken to become a slave later in life
23. Which Greek island was a large marketplace for the buying and selling of slaves during New Testament times? The Island of Delos, located in the Aegean Sea
24. What was the legal status of a Roman slave? Just like an object such as a shoe or sock
25. Why was a runaway slave considered a thief? Because he was stealing (himself) from his master who owned him
26. What Biblical book, written by Paul, discussed a runaway slave named Onesimus? Philemon
27. What was a Roman apartment called? An insulae
28. What was the name of a Roman hot room with a hot plunge bath? A caldarium
29. What was the name of a Roman cold room with a cold plunge bath? A frigidarium
30. What was the largest and most famous Roman amphitheater? The Flavian Amphitheater, also known as the Colosseum
31. Why did gladiators sometimes volunteer? Because those who won sometimes became quite famous and popular
32. How did the Jewish men and women, who were about to be executed in the amphitheater in Rome, pay for the facility in

which they were to die? The Colosseum was funded by spoils from the looted Temple in Jerusalem in AD 70

33. What type of Roman gladiator was named after the Hoplite, a soldier in the Greek phalanx? A hoplomachus
34. What type of Roman gladiator was the most heavily armed? The provocator
35. What type of Roman gladiator used a net as one of his primary weapons? The retiarius
36. For how many centuries did the Roman gladiatorial games take place? Almost seven
37. How did the Tribune in Acts 22 who imprisoned Paul gain his Roman citizenship? He bought it
38. Why did Paul appeal to Caesar when questioned by the Roman procurator Porcius Festus? Because he knew the Jews were going to kill him if he traveled back to Jerusalem
39. Why was exile often encouraged by the Romans for criminals even before their arrest? So the Romans could confiscate their property, and the criminal would not have to be cared for in prison before their trial
40. How many times did the Roman law allow a person be flogged and how did this compare to the Jewish law of flogging? There was no limit for the Romans; the Jews limited the number to 40 (and in practice, they only did 39)
41. Why did the Romans not break the legs of Jesus when he was on the cross as they did the other two men who were crucified with him? Because he was already dead
42. What is the only archaeological evidence we have of someone who had been crucified? A heel bone with a nail through it
43. Why are more nails not found in the archaeological sites showing crucifixion in human remains? Because the Romans reused them
44. What was the name of the only person for which there is archaeological evidence of crucifixion? Jehohanan, son of Hagkol
45. In what year was crucifixion banned in the Roman Empire? Who banned the practice? Emperor Constantine I in AD 337
46. What was the principal unit of the Roman military? The Legion
47. Before the Marius reforms of 107 BC, how many maniples and centuries were there in a legion? 30 maniples and 60 centuries (2 centuries per maniple)

48. What were the three lines that made up the Legion before Marius's reforms? The hastati, the principes, and the triarii

49. After the Marius reforms of 107 BC, how many cohorts and centuries were in a legion? Ten cohorts and 60 centuries (6 centuries per cohort)

50. After the Marius reforms of 107 BC, which cohort and century did the most senior centurion command? The first cohort and the first century in the first cohort

Chapter 16
▪ The Bigger Picture ▪

1. Which are the only three continents the apostles did not evangelize and why? North and South America and Antarctica, because they did not know of them at the time
2. Who was the man chosen to replace Judas Iscariot as an Apostle? Matthias
3. Which of the apostles were fishermen? Peter, Andrew, James and John (and possibly Philip and Bartholomew)
4. From what town were Peter, Andrew, and Philip (and perhaps James and John [the sons of Zebedee])? Bethsaida in Galilee
5. How does tradition say that Peter died? That he was crucified on a cross upside down during the persecutions of Nero
6. Who was the first apostle to be martyred, and how did he die? James, the son of Zebedee, was beheaded by Herod Agrippa I
7. What does "Boanerges" mean, and to whom did this apply? Sons of Thunder—James, and John
8. Which apostle was also known as Nathaniel? Bartholomew
9. What Hebrew name did Matthew also have? Levi
10. Who was the only apostle (of the original twelve) to not be from Galilee? Judas Iscariot
11. In Luke's genealogy of Jesus, what are the two dates and one person we know from other sources? 538 BC when Zerubbabel returned to Jerusalem to rebuild the Temple and 425 BC, the end of the Old Testament
12. Although almost entirely conjecture from Luke's genealogy of Jesus, how many of Jesus's ancestors on Mary's side (including Mary) might have lived in inter-testament times? Fourteen
13. Who is known as the "Father of Medicine" and when did he live? Hippocrates of Cos, 460-377 BC
14. Who is known as the "Father of Zoology" and when did he live? Aristotle of Stagira, 384-322 BC
15. Who tutored the future leaders Alexander the Great, Cassander, and Ptolemy I Soter? Aristotle of Stagira
16. Who is known as the "Father of Botany" and when did he live? Theophrastus of Eresus, 371-287 BC

17. Who is known as the "Father of Geometry" and when was he born? Euclid of Alexandria, 300 BC
18. Who did extensive work with levers and pulleys and said: "give me a place to stand, and I will move the world" and when did he live? Archimedes of Syracuse, 287-212 BC
19. Who determined the circumference of the Earth (at the equator) of about 25,000 miles, which was very close to the actual circumference of 24,901 miles, and when did he live? Eratosthenes of Cyrene, 276-195 BC
20. Who determined the tilt of the earth's axis and when did he live? Eratosthenes of Cyrene, 276-195 BC
21. Who worked out the geometry of conic sections (to the dismay of high school math students everywhere!) and when did he live? Apollonius of Perga, 262-190 BC
22. Who is considered the founder of trigonometry and when did he live? Hipparchus, 190-120 BC
23. Who invented the syringe and when did he live? Heron of Alexandria, AD 10-70
24. Who came up with the concept of latitude and longitude and when did he live? Ptolemy of Alexandrian, AD 90-168
25. What is, arguably, the most famous Roman road, and when did its construction begin? The Appian Way, 312 BC
26. Approximately how many bridges did the Romans build? No less than 900
27. What structure built in Alexandria, Egypt, was considered one of the seven wonders of the ancient world? The Alexandrian lighthouse
28. What event started the Greek period for Judea? When Alexander the Great conquered Persia
29. What event started the Ptolemaic period for Judea? The death of Alexander the Great and Ptolemy I Soter took over Judea
30. What event started the Seleucid period for Judea? The conquest of Judea by Antiochus III the Great
31. What started the Maccabean period? When Mattathias and his sons killed Seleucid officials and started guerilla warfare against Syria
32. When Simon Maccabee was declared "high priest forever," what period for Judea did this start? The Hasmonean period
33. Which Roman leader during the Roman Republic (in 63 BC) began the Roman period for Judea, and how did this happen?

Pompey, who settled a dispute between Hyrcanus II and Aristobulus II

34. When did Josephus write *Wars of the Jews*? AD 71
35. When did Josephus write *Antiquities of the Jews*? AD 94
36. When did Mount Vesuvius erupt? AD 79
37. The transition from the Old Testament period to the inter-testament period happened under which Persian ruler and when did he rule? Artaxerxes I, 464-423 BC
38. Under which puppet Roman king did the transition take place from the inter-testament period to the New Testament period and when did he rule? Herod the Great, 37-4 BC
39. Who were the first and last Roman prefects to rule Judea? Coponius and Marullus
40. Who were the first and final Roman procurators to rule Judea? Cuspius Fadus and Marcus Antonius Julianus
41. It is possible that Antiochus IV Epiphanes and Pontius Pilate did not completely understand why the Jews revolted so much when they attempted cultural changes. Why were these cultural changes an affront to the Jews? They were religious affronts to the Jews, not cultural
42. When the Syrians deposed Onias III as high priest, who outbid him for the office? His brother Jason
43. How much was the Temple tax for every Jewish adult male? One-half shekel
44. What were the three annual attendance-required feasts that took place in Jerusalem? Passover, Feast of Tabernacles, and Pentecost
45. What two languages slowly edged out Biblical Hebrew as the common language of Judea? Aramaic and Greek
46. What main event brought *Aramaic* to Judea? When the Jews returned from Babylonian captivity
47. When did the *Arabic* language start coming on the scene? With the rise of Islam
48. If Jesus was trilingual, what three languages might he have known? Greek, Aramaic, and Hebrew
49. How many sects that existed in inter- and New Testament times still exist today? None
50. From what template have we modeled our Christian churches? Synagogues
51. Instead of the "silent years," what might be a better name for this period? The forgotten years

CPSIA information can be obtained
at www.ICGtesting.com
Printed in the USA
LVHW081026220922
729042LV00012B/352